IN ONE NIGHT

IN ONE NIGHT

KATHY GILBERT

authorHOUSE®

AuthorHouse™
1663 Liberty Drive
Bloomington, IN 47403
www.authorhouse.com
Phone: 1-800-839-8640

Published by AuthorHouse   08/24/2012

ISBN: 978-1-4772-6271-9 (sc)
ISBN: 978-1-4772-6270-2 (e)

Library of Congress Control Number: 2012915194

Any people depicted in stock imagery provided by Thinkstock are models, and such images are being used for illustrative purposes only.
Certain stock imagery © Thinkstock.

This book is printed on acid-free paper.

Because of the dynamic nature of the Internet, any web addresses or links contained in this book may have changed since publication and may no longer be valid. The views expressed in this work are solely those of the author and do not necessarily reflect the views of the publisher, and the publisher hereby disclaims any responsibility for them.

This work is dedicated to
Patricia Ann Hewett
And
William Charlie Hewett.

This is my story about a night that would change my life.

It all started on May 27th, 1961. My mama (Trish) recieved a call from her sister-in-law, Jan that day. Jan wanted to know if she could go with Leah to the dog races in Jacksonville. She was going to go but Lisa, the baby got sick and she can't go. Trish told Jan that she would have to talk to Chad, her husband first. Chad got off work at 3pm. When he got home Trish ask him about going with Leah to the dog races. Chad told her it would be alright and that he would take care of the children. They had four small children, ages ranging from three months to five years old. Trish is a loving, dedicated mother. Chad figured that she could use a little time to unwind and relax. So, she called Jan to let her know that she would go with Leah the next night which was, May the 28th. She was a little excited and nervous because she had not been away from the children in a long time. She knew that Chad would take real good care of them. She cleaned up the house and cooked supper before getting ready to go. She fixed Kathy's favorite meal, spaghetti because she knew that Kathy was going to get upset when she went to leave. Kathy is really close to her mama and is a big helper. Trish set the table and went to get ready. Kathy asked her mama if she could go, but her mama told her that she would have to be daddy's little helper just for tonight. Chad put June in the high chair, Bill at the table and he held Louise, while Trish finished getting ready. Leah pulled up about five, to pick Trish up. Kathy started crying and begging her mama to please let her go. Chad took Kathy by the hand and told her that he needed her to stay to help him with her baby sister. Kathy still wanted to go. She wanted to be with her mama. She watched as they pulled out of the drive way. Trish promised Kathy that she would see her in the morning. Little did any of them know that that would be the last time any of them would see her again. Chad had been up for a few hours because Trish had not come in yet and he had not heard from her. The children got up and wanted to know where their mama was. Chad only told them that their mama was running late. He was already worrying enough and did not want the children upset, no more than they already were. Kathy was real upset that her mama wasn't back like she had promised. Chad already had a bad feeling.

About eight am that morning, he got a call from his brother, Rob. He wanted to know if Trish had made it home.

He told Chad that Trish had called him about 1:30 that morning to ask him how she could get to his house. He told Chad that he told her to stay there and he would be there in ten minutes. She told him that she was at the Shelk station on the corner of Wilson and Blanding Boulevard. But when he got there she was gone. He told Chad that he talked to the attendant on duty, Mr. Bryon. He told Rob that there was two woman there but they left about five minutes before he got there. He told Rob which direction the two women left in. Rob left and went in the direction that the women had gone in. He rode around for awhile but could not locate them. Rob, then went back to talk to Mr. Bryon to see if he could tell him anything else. Chad told Rob that he was going to the Police Station and file a missing person report on May the 29th. He took the children with him to make the report because they just cried so bad when he started to leave so, he got his mama to go with him because he just couldn't leave them. Their heart and his heart was broken enough not knowing where Trish was or if she was alright. Chad knew that something bad had happened, he just didn't know what. On June the first, they filed a missing person report at the Duvell Sheriffs Department. Chad was beside himself with worry. All he wanted was to hear her voice and know that she was alright. On May 30th, a road patrolman, Mr. Bell found Leah's car about 9:43 am that morning. He called in to see if it had been reported stolen. It had not, so he had it stored at Riverglide Impound Company and listed it as unknown. No one knew the car had been found. Chad got his sister-in-law to come stay with them while they searched for Trish and Leah. Aunt Val came and stayed for a few weeks. She had a small baby boy also. She cooked and tried to console the children. They cried alot for their mama. Kathy was just quite. She was withdrawn and didn't play at all. She just sat or stood around as if she was listening to every word the adults were talking about. Chad was worried about her. Chad, Rob and JM, (Leah's brother) met about eight am on June fifth with the detectives. JM told the detectives that Leah liked to play the dogs and that she drank alot. JM also stated that Leah had been despondant since her husband was killed in the war. He also stated that Leah was real paticular about her car. The patrolman, Mr. Bell over heard them talking about the car that he had stored as unknown in the impound garage. He took them to the impound garage so, they could look at the car. When JM saw the car, he knew right away that it was Leah's. It was like a bomb had fell on them. Now they knew something bad had happened.

Mr. Bell told the three men where he had found the car. After leaving the impound garage, the three men went to where the patrolman had found the car. Chad went in one direction and the other two men went in another direction. In a few minutes, the other two men called out to Chad to come here. When he got there, they pointed out another set of tire tracks. After that, they couldn't find anything else, so they left.

The detectives checked Leah's car over throughly. The outside appearence was dirty, the hub caps on the right front and rear wheels were missing. There was mud and sand all over the car. They found grass, like sage grass and mud packed under the fenders, which made it appear the car had been down in some wet ground where it got stuck. The keys were gone and the ignition was in the locked postion. There was also cheese cracker papers on the floor board. They looked in the trunk and it appeared to be intact. The spare tire was flat and it looked as if it had been taken off the left front wheel. The detectives decided to take a closer look at the area where the car was found, for more evidence. The detectives went to talk to Mr. Bryon at the Shelk station. Mr. Bryon told them about the two women. He told them that the younger woman came in to make a phone call and had ask him for some asprins for her headache. He also said that the older woman appeared to be drunk. He also told the detectives that about the same time a dark green pick-up truck had pulled up to the gas pumps. He told them that one of the young men got out and came in the station to get a pack of cigarettes. The other young man stayed in the truck. The young man told him that they were on vacation and was camping down at the river. He then left the store but Mr. Bryon noticed that the young man had stopped and was talking to the older lady in the car. They talked a few minutes, then the young man went to his truck and left going north. Mr. Bryon said that when the younger lady got in the car, that it appeared that the two women were arguing. Mr. Bryon said that the two woman sat there for a few minutes and then left going south. He said that early Tuesday morning the two young men came in and got two dollars worth of gas. He remembered the truck and the one young man that came in for some cigarettes a couple of nights before. Chad went back home to be with his children. They cried for their mama but he didn't know what to tell them. He didn't have any answers at all. He wished that Trish would walk in the door and announce that she was back but he had given up hope of that happening since they had found Leah's car. Chad was so thankful for Val being there to help him with the children. He wasn't sleeping much. He couldn't get his mind off Trish. Oh, how he loved her. He missed her more than anyone realized. Trish was his whole heart. Val was doing a good job but she wasn't the childrens mother. Chad tried to console the children but it didn't help much and Kathy wasn't herself. She was like a totally different little girl. She didn't play or say to much to anyone. He worried about her the most and what this was doing to her. She wouldn't talk to him no matter how hard he tried to get her to open up to him. He hoped he knew something soon about Trish, good or bad, he needed to know. He tried to work but he couldn't keep his thoughts off of Trish. So, he tried to help look for Trish and Leah.

Chad's family rallied around him and the children. Trying to make things a little easier for him. They helped cook, clean, play with the children and to keep up with his bills, to make sure they didn't get behind. Chad was so glad his family was there for him. He didn't know what he would do without them. Every second of the day, he was worrying about Trish and Leah. Wondering where they were and if they were okay. He prayed an awful lot that God would bring them home safely. Trish and Leah had been missing for almost two weeks. It didn't look good for either of them.

The FBI had the river dragged for bodies but they only found Trish's billfold and no other evidence was found. On the afternoon of June 6th, the FBI got in touch with the detectives. They told them that they were going to get a helicopter to go up and look around the area where the car was found. Hoping they would see some kind of evidence from up in the air. They told the detectives to meet with them where the car was found at 9 am, the next morning.

The FBI went up in the helicopter at about 9. There was three detectives on the ground, so when the helicopter would relay something to the ground patrol, they would check it out. At 10:30 am on June the seventh the FBI in the helicopter observed the bodies of the women almost west of where their car was found. The bodies were lying parallel to each other about four feet apart. The body that was identified as Leah, was lying face down with her arms extended above her head. She was partially clothed from the waist up and from the waist down she was naked. They found a dark blue skirt with a lighter blue stripe with small prints of flowers, green and orange, next to her. She had been missing for almost two weeks in the heat, so her body was partially decomposed. To the left of Leah, was Trish's body. Her arms also extended above her head. She was fully clothed but with one white high heel shoe on her right foot. The other shoe was found about 30 feet north of the body. Trish's body was badly decomposed plus some of the wild animals had got a hold of both the women. The bodies were viewed where they found them and sent to Duville County Morgue, where they performed an autopsy on both of the women. When they did the autopsy on Trish, they found a brass key on a chain between her clothing and her upper right shoulder. She was badly decomposed. Several areas on her head were peeling from the scalp. The skin on her lower jaw was gone and showed her teeth. The remaining skin of the arms, trunk and face is black and appears mumified. Only twenty-five percent of the skin remains on the body. There was maggots all over both bodies.

Chad realized that if his brother hadn't called him back that day, that he would have walked up on the bodies. He had been twenty-five feet from them. He thanked God that he had not found them that day. Because he knew if he had, that they would have had to bury him also. Chad was contacted to come down to identify the body. His brother, Rob, Val and his other brother that was kin to Leah (Henry) came with him. Chad couldn't do it so, Val and Rob identified Trish's body. But they told Chad that he would never have closure, if he didnt go look for himself to see if it was really her. So, after a couple of hours they convinced Chad to go in to see for himself. Chad and Henry went in. When Chad saw for certain that it was Trish, he fell all apart. His world came crashing down on him. He could not get a hold of himself for quite awhile. His family tried to console him but it didn't help much. He had lost the love of his life and the mother of his children. What was he going to tell them and how?

How was he gonna take care of his children without their mama? They were already going through enough. His family saw that he got home safe. The children ran to him and ask, "have they found our mommy yet"? That just tore him apart but he had to be strong for them. He explained to them that their mama had gone to Heaven to be with Jesus. That Jesus needed her to be one of his angels. Oh, how they cried. Kathy just walked off and cried all by herself. She wanted her mama. After she was told that her mama wasn't coming back, she really withdrew. She would never be the same. Kathy just blocked it all out.

Chad brought Trish's body back to Valdosta to Landies Funeral Home. It was gonna have to be closed casket because of the decomposure. It was a sad time for the family. The children were there. Chad had to be so strong but he broke down listening to his children crying for their mama to come back. It was so hard on the whole family on both sides. Chad had some difficult decisions to make. For now, Val would stay till he made other arrangements but she was going to have to go back to her own home soon.

The FBI were still investigating the scene where they found the bodies and where they found the car. They found a place where a car had turned around and about 30 feet west of where the tire marks were located, it seemed that the car had knocked some bark from a small sapling pine tree. They took a piece of bark and some dirt for evidence. The location where the bodies were found appeared to be an old woods road. The grass looked like some vehicle had pulled through there. That road ran north. Thirty feet from the bodies, south, another road ran off to the west. They found one white garter fifteen feet from the west of this junction. They found a pair of white torn panties in the road on the south lane approximately 25 feet from the first garter. They found another white garter ten feet west of the pair of panties in the road. Near where the last garter was found there was a fifteen foot tire track on the north side of the road where the tire had skidded as if the vehicle had started up in a hurry, heading east. Then about a hundred-fifteen feet west of the last garter and fifteen feet south of the road, they found a small cloth belt loop, colored dark blue as if it had been torn off a piece of clothing. Sixty feet south of the tire marks, they found earlier, in a heavy grass section, they found an olive green, woman's corduroy left shoe with a black shoe string still tied. They believed the shoe belonged to Leah. In the area where the torn panties were found, a cigarette butt was found. As of now the brand was undetermined.

They got in touch with Chad to see if Trish had any jewlery. Chad said that Trish wore a yellow gold engagment ring with one large diamond and two smaller ones on each side and also a yellow gold wedding band with three small chip diamonds. Chad said she also wore a man's yellow gold round wrist watch with a gold expansion band with two small leather sections on each side. The face is also gold. Leah was wearing a yellow gold engagement ring with a small diamond in the center and also a yellow gold wedding band with three or four diamonds in it. She also wore a yellow gold Air Force ring with a blue stone in it. Her watch was yellow gold believed to be a bulava with a small round face. Leah's brother-in-law told them that she also had a 38-calibre Smith and Wesson revolver with a brown handle and a 4 inch barrel. He said that she kept it in the glove box of her car. The detectives and the FBI could not find any jewelry or the pistol. When they did the autopsy, a womans stocking was tied around both womens necks and tied in a bow to the front of their clothes. It was ruled as asphyxiation due to stragulation. There was evidence that Leah was raped but Trish was not. The reason believed to be was because Trish was on her period. Now, they were looking for a dirty, dark green international pick up truck that came in the station at the same time as the two women. The truck had an Arkansaw tag and two young men were driving the truck when last seen. After the funeral, Chad

had made the decision to move in with his Mom, so that she could help with the children, especially with three month old Louise. Trish had been dead for a month and Val had to go back to her home, so she could take care of her baby son. So, everyone chipped in and helped Chad get everything packed up and moved into his mother's house. The children still missed their mother but they were coping. Little Kathy was still withdrawn. She would not remember the funeral or moving to her grandmothers. She would play sometimes but most of the time she just sat listening to the grown-ups. As if she could understand what they were talking about and maybe she understood more than anyone realized. Chad was hoping that she would come around eventually. His mother was very stricked with the children, especially with Kathy, he believed that it was because she looked alot like her mama. His mama wasn't fond of his deceased wife. Life went on and things got a little easier. Chad went back to work, it helped to keep his mind busy. Kathy would go stay with her Aunt Jan on weekends sometimes which made her happy. She use to believe that her Aunt Jan was her mama. She only vaguely remembers staying with her for a short period of time, after her mama died.

On June 10th, 1962, the two boys that was driving the dark green pick-up truck was arrested in Toole County, violating the Federal National Motor Vehicle Theft Act which prohibited transportation of a stolen vehicle across state lines. On June 12th of 1962, Parker and Levi bragged to the investigaters that they had killed nine people since they had left Fort Hoop. They laughed about killing the two women;said that they wanted to see which one would die first, the drunk or the sober one. Then, they made a comment that they did all those people a favor by taking them out of this old world. They said the world was getting bad.

Police later learned that out of the nine people believed to have been killed, two had survived. The boys claimed that being placed in a mixed race unit, led to their desire to desert the Army. There is six states fighting for these two boys that went across their states killing. Kansas got to take them to trial.

Chad and some family members went to Kansas but the guards wouldn't let them in the court room as they were afraid trouble would break out. They had to stand outside the courtroom while the trial was going on. The jury sentenced the two boys to hang by the neck till dead, on December 19th, 1962. The two boys were not tried for the other murders that they commited. But the boys admitted to killing the two women in Florida, as they admitted to all the rest of the killings across the six states. So, that left the rest of the cases opened because the boys were not tried for each murder. The boys appealed to the courts, till they ran out of options. So, on June the 22nd, 1965, they were hanged. Kathy was staying at her Aunt Jan's when it came on the news about the boys and her mama. She wouldn't move to tell her aunt because she was afraid that she would miss what they said. Her Aunt Jan came in as it went to commercial and Kathy told her aunt all about it. When the news came back on they didn't mention anything else about the boys or her mama. They were the last two to be hung in Kansas. The two young men were well dressed and nice looking young men. To look at them, you would not believe that they were capable of murder. They destoried so many lives by their actions. Especially the children that had to grow up without a mother. Other families missing their dad, brother or daughter. Chad was glad that justice was served. Now, maybe he could have closure. He still missed Trish very much, she would always be the love of his life. The children were doing better. Kathy was still alittle withdrawn but not as bad. He prayed she would come around and have a normal life or one close to it. Sometimes they would go visit a great uncle. Kathy didn't like going there because he would touch her in places that he should not. Kathy was afraid to tell anyone so, she kept it to herself. Kathy got scared of all old men. Every weekend, Chad would take the kids to Dan and Julie's to let them play and be kids. Dan had four kids and so did he. Dan and his wife, Julie had been friends with him and Trish for a long time. The kids would get up in the barn where they would play in the corn that was stored there to feed the hogs. That was so much fun. Kathy and the girls would look for wild violets in the woods. The woods were clear enough they could see where they were going. That was the place that Kathy was the happiest in her childhood. All the children had to play outside. They weren't allowed in the house except to eat and use the bathroom. If it rained, they would let them play in the kids bedroom. Kathy had great memories there. She would go back there even after she was grown. At the age of twelve, Kathy was sent to stay awhile with her third cousin, who was going to have a baby that summer. When her cousin wasn't around, her cousin's husband would corner Kathy and french kiss her. At that time Kathy had no idea what it was called. It scared her and she tried to stay right up under her cousin. Kathy couldn't understand why her cousin couldn't see how scared she was. Kathy put in to go home and they took her home but carried her eight year old sister back with them. He molested her also and she told her Aunt Jan. Her Aunt Jan told their daddy. Talking about mad, boy was he. He went to his cousin-n-law and punched him in the face. He hit him so hard that it knocked him down and he weighed about three hundred pounds and Chad weighed about one - seventy. He then told him that he was to never go near his girls again, that the next time he would kill him. Chad knew that his children had been through enough, without having to go through more trama. Chad saw how Kathy was being treated by his mama, he didn't like it and so he promised her that when she got old enough to help him take care of a place, that he would get them a home of their own. He kept his promise, when Kathy turned 13, he found them a trailer not to far from his parents. Chad hired someone to watch the children till he got off of work at 11:30 at night. The children seemed to be doing better since they had their own home. Kathy loved her daddy so much. She worked really hard at keeping the house cleaned. She wanted him to be so proud of her but what she didn't know was that he really was proud of her. He just didn't tell her that very often. Kathy would spend her weekends with her Aunt Jan. She loved her so much. But she still missed her mama. Sometimes she cried silently, so no one would hear her crying for her mama. When she would cry, she would beg her mama to come to her and one night she did. Kathy felt a hand on her shoulder as she laid there crying and calling for her mama, at first it startled her but all of a sudden, she was calm. She put her hand where she could feel the hand on her shoulder and went to sleep. It was the first time that she experienced that. It made her happy and she felt at peace because she knew that that was her mama touching her shoulder. That she had come to her, to let her know that she loved her and everything was going to be okay. Kathy still missed her deeply. Her daddy was good to her but he wouldn't get close to her. Kathy didn't understand why he couldn't get close to her like she wanted. She wanted a father- daughter relationship. She would find out later in her life why he wouldn't allow himself to get close to her. He did depend on her to help him. At age 15, Kathy got a part time job just so she could help him alittle more. She loved him so much. She worship the ground he walked on and only wanted him to be happy. Chad missed Trish as much as Kathy did. They both was hurting on the inside but on the outside they seemed to be fine.

Kathy had questions about her mama, so she decided to ask her daddy. She ask him what her mama's favorite flower was and he told her that it was a yellow rose but she noticed how sad he was and vowed to never hurt him again by asking questions about her mama. Kathy felt so bad because she had made her daddy so sad. Chad lived for his children. They were his pride and joy. He just wanted them to have as close a normal life as they could, since they were without a mama. He took them to the grave site with him every weekend.

Kathy would watch him take out his pocket knife and cut the grass away from the head stone. He would look so sad. She noticed him talking to her, too. They would only stay for a short time. While he cut the grass away from the head stone, they would go to where the statue of Jesus was and the gold fish. Kathy loved to go there to look at the gold fish and to read the verse under Jesus's feet. It read, "Whosoever shall believeth in me shall have ever lasting life. "Kathy believed in Jesus because her mama was with him, as one of his angels. Chad wrecked his car and didn't know how he was gonna make ends meet. Kathy over heard him talking about the bills. The next day, she went to where she was working part time and talked to the manager about going to work full time. The manager told her that she had needed someone full time. Kathy dropped out of school, and helped her daddy take care of the bills and the younger children. She enjoyed helping her daddy and she loved working. Christmas was coming and Chad knew that he wouldn't be able to get any presents for the smaller children, so he went to Kathy. He ask her if she would mind buying Christmas for the family. Kathy felt full of happiness and pride that her daddy had ask her to do this for him. She found out what each one really wanted and that was the special gift that she bought them besides other things. She wanted to do something special for her daddy, so she bought him a Father's ring with all their birthstones in it, including his and her mama's. When she got her last pay check, Chad came and asked her for it. She asked him why he wanted her last pay check and he told her that everyone had presents but her. That he wanted to get her something to open on Christmas. It was a great Christmas, everyone loved their gifts. Especially Kathy, her daddy had bought her an 8 track player. Kathy treasured it. Chad got back on his feet, with her help and she was glad that her daddy seemed to be happier . In 1973, Kathy married Dakota. At first they were happy. They had moved to Albany but had come back to see their families. Kathy had went to the doctor to see if she was pregant. Her and Dakota got into a bad arguement at his mama's house, she left walking. Dakota picked her up and took her to her daddy's and told her to get out. She felt like she was nothing, a failure and couldn't tell her daddy for fear that she had let him down. So, she went in, found the sleeping pills that belonged to her daddy. He didn't take them because they were to strong for him but Kathy didn't know this. Kathy took about four but something kept telling her to drop the other pill that she was going to take down the drain. She did, then she went to her daddy's neighbors house and told her what she had done. They called the doctor and he told them to get her to the hospital as fast as they could. Kathy's brother came up and Helen told Bill what Kathy had done. Helen and Bill put Kathy in the car and rushed her to the hospital. Before they could get her to the hospital, Kathy was already out. When she got there, they pumped her stomach out. It would be hours before Kathy would come out of it completely. The doctor told her daddy not to let her go to sleep because she might not wake up. Kathy remembers her sisters begging her not to go to sleep. They also put her in a cold shower, to help keep her awake. She wouldn't remember much at all but she learned a valuable lesson that day. That nothing or nobody was worth killing yourself over. She also wanted to go to Heaven and knew if she had died that she would not have gone to Heaven. Then she found out that she was pregant about a month after her atempted suicide. They had been married about ten months, when the violent side of him started showing. She was seven months pregant, when he tried to push her down in the tub. Once he started the violence, he kept right on. He wouldn't hold a job and they had to move in with her daddy. He didn't know about the abuse and Kathy dared not tell him for fear that he would be disappointed in her. She always worried about what her daddy would think about her. She had little Mat in Febuary and Dakota was working at the meat plant. Mat was only three weeks old, when they got a trailer next to her daddy. One night, Dakota flipped crazy and threatened to throw Mat up side the wall. Kathy was scared that he would do it and begged him to give her the baby. Mat had a tummy ache and that was why he crying. Dakota put him under the water faucet to try to make him shut up. Kathy begged him to give her the baby, telling him that she could get him to stop crying. Finally, he gave Kathy the baby and she got him eased off enough for him to go to sleep. He told her to go next door to their friends house to get him a cigarette. She took Mat with her because she was afraid that he would wake up and she didn't know what Dakota would do. So, while she was there, she called her cousin, Jennie and ask her if she could come get her and Mat. Jennie told her that she would be there about 10 am the next morning to pick up her and the baby. Kathy got up so she could get Dakota up for work. Mat woke up cranky and Dakota started talking about staying home. Kathy told him that he needed to go to work so he wouldn't loose his job. He agreed. Dakota left for work and Kathy started packing a few things. When Jennie got there she told Kathy that they were getting everything. After they got everything loaded, they left. They went by their grandmother's house, where her aunts and uncles were. They noticed the bruises on Mat's back where Dakota had patted him to get him to quite down. Kathy took him to the hospital where they xrayed Mat to make sure there wasn't any damage done to him. Kathy and Mat went to South Carolina to stay with her aunt and uncle. When she got there, Kathy went to looking for a job. She got a job at a shirt factory. She, then looked for a good baby sitter. There was a lady who lived down the street from where she lived who was really good with children. Kathy loved her job. She was so proud of herself. That she was working and taking care of Mat. Then her aunt started talking to her about going out with her brother, Tom. He had lost his wife in a tragic accident. Tom had a five year old daughter, who Kathy liked alot. Kathy was 18 years of age and Tom was 36 years of age. They dated for a short time. They were happy and did family things together. But her aunt started accusing her of things that weren't true. One night, her and Kathy had a bad arguement over Kathy's son and her aunts brother, Tom. After that, Kathy stayed to herself. She would go to work and stay in her room with Mat. She would come out to take a bath, bathe Mat and eat supper. She stopped seeing Tom, thinking that would make her aunt happy but it didn't. She got a message to Dakota, to come get her. She didn't know what else to do. In a couple of days, Dakota was there. She couldn't take everthing, so she packed as many clothes for her and Mat as she could. She wanted to take a few things that meant the world to her like her eight track player but she wasn't able to, since they were going to have to carry everything on the bus. It was a long ride back to Georgia. But Dakota seemed to be happy to see her and Mat. Kathy never did get to get any of her things from her aunts house and later learned that her aunt gave all her things away to her side of the family. Including her eight track player that her daddy got her. Her aunt knew what that meant to her. When Mat was a year old, Dakota started pushing Kathy around and sometimes, he would make her sit in the dark in a corner in the kitchen with a knife stuck at her side, daring her to get up. He wouldn't let her go see about Mat, if he cried. He would break her things and make her clean them up. He would talk crazy things. She learned later that he had been taking some kind of pills that made him talk out of his head. She was scared of him. After a year and a half, she had her second child, Lee. But she wouldn't tell nobody how Dakota treated her. For fear that they would think it was all her fault.

One morning Mat, who was almost three decided that he wanted to go see his Papa. So, he slipped out of the house and went to go see his Papa. He had to cross a four lane highway and go two and a half blocks from there. He had almost made it there when the Police officers picked him up. He only lacked a half of a block. In the mean time, Kathy was in a panic and had the whole neighborhood looking for him and on top of it all, it was raining. A policeman brought Mat to her and told her what a sorry mother she was. Kathy felt like the worst mama in the world. What they didn't know was that Kathy had been tending to Lee, who was only a couple of weeks old and didn't think that Mat could get that far, let alone get out the front door. Dakota got a job on a hog farm but he would only bring twenty dollars home on pay day and tell Kathy that that was all he made. The boss man furnished them with housing and electicity. There was times that Kathy only had enough food for the children and Dakota. So, she would eat lard with sugar on it to keep from being hungary. She made sure that her children were fed. Chad found out that his daughter was eating lard and sugar, he showed up at her house with several bags of groceries. He told Kathy that the next time she better call him for help. Kathy was ashamed to call him for help. Kathy thanked him and told him that she would call him next time. But she prayed that there would be no next time. She had always been a fighter and could hold her ground but she never had to fight a man. After about two years, Kathy found her backbone. She learned how to fight a man real fast. Dakota didn't know what to think the first time Kathy started fighting back. Then, Kathy caught him with other women. They had fights about that too, because he would be mad that Kathy would know about the other women, dates and places that they would meet. He couldn't understand how she knew those things. What he didn't know was that alot of her friends knew him but he didn't know them. After about six years of this, Kathy met

Walter. He was Louise's brother-n-law. He liked Kathy and was there for her. They had an affair for a couple of months, until Kathy got scared that Dakota would find out and kill her. She really loved Walter but couldn't take a chance on being hurt or killed like her mama. Then she found out that she was expecting her third child. She wasn't sure if Dakota or Walter was the father but she wasn't going to say anything. Walter moved to Texas after that. She had alittle girl, who she named, Jessica. She didn't hear from Walter until Jessica was two and a half. He came back and looked Kathy up. By this time, Kathy believed that Jessica was Walter's daughter. Dakota was always gone. They had seperated because he had another woman. Walter came to see how Kathy was doing. She decided to tell him that Jessica was his but he didn't take the news to good. He was still a young man, who was only ninteen. Kathy assured him that there was no strings attached. She still loved him but she knew that he wasn't ready to settle down. He was only in town for about two weeks and he went back to Texas. Kathy would never know for sure who the father of Jessica was. When Mat was seven, the Department of family and children services stepped in. They took Mat away from Kathy. She fought so hard to get him back. Dakota made things worst. The department of Family and Children services talked them both into signing a blank piece of paper, explaining to them that it would have their agreement on their visitation and marriage counseling on it. After about six months they took Lee and Jessica. They wanted Kathy to sign adoption papers on Mat but she wouldn't, then they wanted her to divorce Dakota. Kathy divorced Dakota, so she could have her children back. She didn't know alot about her rights as she was only twenty-five. Things like that no one discussed. She was devastated when they took her other two children, especially since she was doing everything they were telling her to do. Kathy missed her children so bad that she turned to alchol but she went to work every day. She kept her house and kept plenty of groceries in it. She paid her bills like she was suppose to do. She kept her visitations with her children. She had no one. Her daddy, Chad had passed away a year after Jessica was born. Three days after Kathy buried her daddy, she had a dream. She dreamed that her daddy was laying in the casket and she was crying over him, asking him if he knew just how much she loved him. Her daddy sat up in the casket, got out and put his arm around Kathy and told her that he knew how much she loved him. She woke up and knew that everything was going to be okay. How she wished that she could talk to her daddy just one more time. After her daddy died, her daddy's neighbor told Kathy that the reason her daddy couldn't get close to her was because he was afraid that the same thing that happened to her mama, would happen to her. So, she when it came time to go to court, she went all by herself. She was so scared because she didn't know what to expect. Her lawyer convienantly had a town meeting outside of town. She called legal aid to see if they could represent her but no one could help her. When she got to the courthouse she told the case worker that she was going to ask for a postponement and that she was fighting for all three of her children. She got to see Mat for a few minutes before court started. When they got in there, she didn't know when she could speak to the judge. But before she could speak to the judge, the welfares lawyers started on Mat's case. The judge looked at Kathy and told her that she could have Lee and Jessica back but he was dissolving her parenting rights to Mat. The judge never ask her where or if she had any legal representitive. She couldn't understand how they could take her child from her, when she loved and fought for him so hard. Afterwards Kathy asked to see Mat, but they would not let her see him. She was devastated that she had lost Mat and did not understand what had happened. Part of her heart was missing but she was going to take good care of her other two children. After she got her children back, she didn't drink another drop. Even, after she got her two children back, the department of family and children services still harrassed her. They had her nerves shot to the point that she had to see a therapist. The therapist told them they could only go see Kathy if she was persent. She lived in fear that they would come get her children again every day. She was afraid to spank them and other options didn't work. The Department of Family and children services came to her house about fifty times and never could find anything wrong. No neglate, no abuse, the house was always clean no matter when they showed up. There was plenty of food in the house and their play area was safe.

Kathy remarried after she had been divorced about a year. Tim was good to her and loved her alot. But after two years, she realized that she had married on rebound. They were happy but she wasn't in love with Tim. She had a job as a waitress at a local restraunt. She loved her job. Her old flame Walter, came back into town. He was seeing a married woman and her husband shot him in the foot. After that, he looked up Kathy to see her and they decided to move in together. Walter's foot wasn't healing right, so Kathy made him a poldise like her granny taught her and put it on the bottom of his foot. Next morning, when they took the bandage off, there was a piece of the bullet in the bandage. After that, it healed up fine. Walter started cheating on her with one of his old flames and he started abusing her. They moved to Adel, Kathy had always liked that town. Her Aunt Jan lived in Sparks, which was only a mile from Adel. They were together about two years but he beat and cheated on her too. He had pulled a gun on her once. He was also an alcholic. When they moved to Adel, Kathy decided that she had had all the abuse that she was gonna take. So, she left him. After almost two years, Walter had destoried all the love that she had had for him for twelve years. She was working at the truck stop as a waitress there. She found a trailer for her and her two children. Louise was living in the same trailer park. They helped each other and was there for one another. Kathy loved her sister's and her brother very much. Kathy's best friend, Amy introduced her to Ken. He was from up north but had moved down here a couple of years ago. He had family here. Kathy and Ken started dating. After about a month, they decided to move in together. They had so much in common. He loved the children and they loved him. Ken took up time with them and played games with them. He was a daddy to them that they never had. Kathy fell in love with him and him with her. They were so happy together. Ken was a hard working man. After about two months, Ken ask Kathy to marry him. But Ken had a dark secret that Kathy didn't know about. It would be eleven years before she would know for sure how bad it was. Ken got into alittle trouble which he told Kathy that the drugs were the other man's but he was with him, so they charged him too. He had to spend six months in a detention center. Kathy was working, so she paid the bills and planned their wedding. Dale, a friend of theirs was renting a room from them, so the extra money helped. Dale also paid Kathy to wash his clothes. Jessica had her first baby on the fourteenth of June and Ken got out of the detention center the sixteenth. They were buying a double wide trailer, so they planned their wedding outside for the seventh of July. Kathy had always wanted a real wedding.

Kathy's favorite color was purple and that was going to be her wedding colors. She had a real wedding cake. It was three tiers, white with purple roses, white beads and doves all around it. Her son, Lee was going to walk her down the isle and her daughter (Jessica) was going to be one of the brides maid. Her best friend, Tammy was her maid of honor and her other friend Kelly was a brides maid also. It was a beautiful wedding and the day was perfect. Ken's Mom and two of his aunts came down from up north for the wedding. Kathy was so excited that Mertle was there, she loved her like she was her own mama. She was also pleased that Aunt Beth and Aunt Cindy could also be there. So, after almost eight years, Kathy and Ken was finally married. Kathy got to have a real wedding instead of a court house wedding. Ken's mama (Mertle) and Kathy had gotten really close. It was like a mother and daughter relationship from the start. They had a wonderful life but Kathy still didn't know his dark secret. Both Lee and Jessica dropped out of school after Kathy took them on her jobs and told them to get an education, so that they wouldn't have to work manual labor like she did. After they dropped out they didn't want to work either. Jessica got pregant and had a little boy that she named Sam. Sam was Kathy's heart, she took up alot of time with him. Jessica, (Jake) the babies daddy and Lee all lived with her and Ken. None of them was working. Lee finally got a job. Then Lee got into some minor trouble and had to go to a detention center for six months. Kathy had not forgotten about Mat. She looked for him for many years before she would finally find him. After they had been married for three years, Ken cheated on her with one of her best friends, Patty, so she thought. She had asked them several times if anything was going on between the two of them. But they both told her that they loved her and would never hurt her like that ever. They just kept on lying to her face. Ken finally came clean.

In 2002, Kathy found Mat. He was doing time in prison for crimmal trespassing. She hunted him for almost eighteen years before she found him. When he got out, he moved to Sparks to be closer to his mama. She borrowed the money to get him a trailer. She bought and gave him all the things that he would need to take care of himself. Enough food for a month but he didn't want to work either. He met a wonderful woman, who he had a little girl with, that they named Lynda. She was a pretty little thing and looked just like her daddy. Kathy loved Lynda and she was a good baby. Kathy was proud of her children and her grandchildren. Mat and Aierl broke up. She met someone else who killed her because he was jealous of her. It was a very sad time, especially for Kathy because it brought back the emptiness that she had felt when her mama died. Her heart went out to Lynda. She was only three years old and would never get to know her mama. Aierl's mama would raise Lynda. But they all stayed in Lynda's life. Mat met another wonderful woman that already had kids which Kathy loved just the same.

By this time, Kathy knew the truth about Ken's secret. Ken had a bad drug problem. He was hooked on crack so bad that he would steal money from Kathy or blow his whole paycheck sometimes. He only blew his pay check once every couple of months. Kathy tried to help him but he couldn't be helped. Then she got a call from someone telling her to ask Ken about another woman named Sue. She asked Ken but he lied about knowing her. So, she decided to investigate on her own. By the time Ken got home from working out of town, Kathy had all the details. She confronted him and he finally told her all about it but he said that it was just a place to go do his drug so she wouldn't know how much he was doing. They lost their double wide trailer because of the drugs and him not paying the payment. Kathy found a house six miles in the country and the rent was cheap. Ken got even worse on the crack. He had started shooting it up but Kathy didn't know this as of yet. Lee had met a wonderful woman and they were together. She already had a grown son and a twelve year old daughter. To Lee, those were his kids. April was a wonderful woman and Kathy really liked her. She made Lee a better man. Jessica had got with Dale and they had a little boy named Brent. Kathy loved all her grandchildren and step grandchildren. Kathy thought that her and Ken had worked out all their problems. But she didn't know that he was seeing a woman that would do the drug with him. She was on the drug as bad as he was and would do whatever it took to get more.

About a year after they moved into the house in the country, Ken walked out on Kathy because the drug had took him and he wanted to be with the other woman. Kathy was devastated. She loved him so much. But, he had left her six miles in the country, no way to go, no job and all the bills. Kathy was a fighter and didn't give up easily at all. She was determined to make it and to move on. Ken was the first person that she had ever gave her whole heart too. She felt like it shattered to pieces that day when he walked out on her. Kathy didn't like to ask for help, she tried to do things on her on. But she wasn't going to be able to do that this time. So, she swallowed her pride and called her Aunt Jan, to see if she could borrow her car to go find a job. Her aunt couldn't drive any more, so she let Kathy borrow the car but she could only look for work in their town. Kathy got a job at the Fairy Dream. She put in forty or fifty hours a week and cleaned houses after she got off work there. Kathy packed his duffle bag with as many of his clothes as she could. He had left his cigarettes and his billfold which she packed in the duffle bag. She put it in the swing on the front porch. She changed all the locks so that he couldn't get in because she was afraid he would steal everything that she had worked hard for. Tammy, her best friend moved in with her but she only stayed there sometimes. It was an old house with no insulation, so it was cold in there, even with heaters. It was in Decemeber and it had been a cold winter sure enough.

Kathy came home to find her hammer laying on the table. She knew that she had not put it there and then she noticed the light was on in her bedroom. She turned it off and walked into the living room, where she saw that someone had kicked in the front door and had tried to fix it back. She saw her movies were all messed up and about fifty or sixty of them was gone. Kathy called the police. They came out and investigated and found one of the DVD players was also gone.

Kathy felt like she had been violated. That's the only way she could describe how she felt. The officer told Kathy that there was nothing they or she could do as long as her and Ken was married. That he could break into her house no matter where she moved to and take whatever he wanted to. Kathy was so upset to hear that. She called her children and friends to help her move her things into a storeage unit. She called her boss man and told him what happened and ask if she could have two days off to get everything packed and put in storage. Her boss man gave her the two days off. In those two day she had packed everything and got everything into storage. She only kept some clothes, her small stereo, her small tv and her personal items. She moved in with Tammy and her sister but they got evicted the next day. So, Kathy moved in with her daughter, Jessica. At first it was okay. Then Dale, Jessica's husband who was an alcholic, started showing his true colors around Kathy and she didn't like it. Kathy started looking for a cheap place to rent. An old landlord came in where she worked. She asked him if he had anything to rent but he told her that he had gotten out of the rental business. He then told her that he had a trailer that he would sell to her for a dollar. Kathy couldn't believe it. They met at the trailer park where the trailer was. All the windows had tin over them but one, because someone had busted the glass out. He had the doors screwed shut and there was a big hole in the kitchen floor, it had an old screw in fuse box and the hot water heater was no good. Kathy told him that she would buy it. So, the papers were drawn up and signed but he wouldn't take her dollar. Told her he wished her the best. Kathy knew it needed alot of work. She stayed with Jessica, hoping she could get some help on fixing her trailer. Every evening, when Dale got home, he started drinking. He would walk around giving these evil looks, slamming cabinets and doors. Just trying to start an argument. Then, he wanted to fight and Jessica was one that wouldn't back down. She fought like a man. Kathy would stay in her room till she heard them fighting and the kids crying. She would try to get them to stop but you can't make a drunk see reason. Dale would tell her that she had to find somewhere else to go or just tell her to get out. He told her this a few times and Kathy got all her things together. The last time, he told her that, she got everything that belonged to her and left. She moved into her trailer. Her friends, Amy and Roger tried to get her to come stay at there house but Kathy told them that she was tired of packing her things up and unpacking them. That that was her trailer and no one could tell her to get out. She moved in her trailer the second week in July. Amy would let her take a bath at their house and they loaned her a big cooler. Kathy would make a pitcher of tea at Amy's house to put in the cooler, so she would have something to drink. She bought food to eat and kept it in the cooler. She bought ice everyday. Kathy filled two five gallon buckets up with water from Amy's, so she could flush the toilet and to wet a rag to keep cool at night and to bathe off, when she didn't go to Amy's to get a shower. She had her phone transfered to her trailer just in case she needed help and to talk to her mom. Kathy stayed in her trailer for two weeks without electricity. Roger, Amy,

the Pastor and some of the church members got together to pay to have Kathy's electric and water turned on. Kathy came home and cried when she saw what they had done for her. Then, Roger got some of his friends to come over and they put the living room and kitchen windows in. They looked so good and Kathy was so thankful. Roger got Ken to come help him put her kitchen floor down. After they got the floor down, they laid the tile down. After they had finished the floor, they put her stove and refridgerator in the trailer. When Kathy got home from work, she was amazed. Her trailer was beginning to look like a real home. In her spare time, she painted the front bedroom a beautiful blue, her bedroom a purple because it was her favorite color, the kitchen a lemon yellow and brown. She put Chef Dude border around the top of the walls in the kitchen. The trailer was beginning to look like a new one. She finally got Dale to come cut the rest of the boards, so she could finish all the floors. Then, she laid the tile on the rest of the floor and laid carpet in the living room.

What she made at the Fairy Dream, she paid bills with and what she made cleaning houses was what she bought her materials that her trailer needed. Lee came over to put her hot water heater in and repiped her bathroom. Another friend came and put the breaker box in. Kathy put new locks on the front door. The back door, she left screwed shut. She was so proud of her home and so thankful. Kathy went and got her things out of storage. In the process of unloading her stuff, a box went missing with her game cube, controllers, games, the old nitendo system, a game boy advance, vcr and a clock was in it. Come to find out, a friends husband stole it while they were helping her unload her stuff. He sold the things to a store in Valdosta. Her friend brought the vcr back and told her what her husband did. Kathy told her if she got her stuff back that she wouldn't press charges. So, they got some of the games, the controllers, and the game cube back but she didn't get the other things. Kathy felt like she had been violated again.

Her friend, Tammy got her a job with her, making alot better pay. She had paid off all her bills except her living expenses. She gave two weeks notice to the Fairy Dream and on June nineth, went to work with a Fat Pup team. She reset the Fat Pup shelves. It was a grocery store chain. Kathy worked fifteen stores in ten different towns. She loved it and made the most money that she had ever made in her life at any job. She was proud of herself and her family was proud of her. Ken moved in with her next door neighbor Don, with the woman that he left her for. That about broke her heart, till she finally decided to tell him good bye for good. She only wanted to be friends with them both. She wanted to go to heaven so, she forgave them. After she did that, her life got better and she was happier. One week out of the month, she would stay in Florida because they had three stores there and one in Cairo. She enjoyed that because she had two really good friends with her. One was her best friend that she had had for seventeen years and the other was a good friend of ten years. Kathy opened up a bank account and saved her money. She paid what bills she had and once in a while she would splurge and buy a couple of movies or a new outfit to wear. Kathy would go out with the girls on Saturday night dancing. She loved that. She was their designated driver. Her life was so much better since she told Ken goodbye and they were just friends. Ken and his girlfriend, Tina had hit rock bottom and now they were getting their life together. But it took them three years of doing the crack and going to prison before they got it under control. They got married not long after Kathy told Ken goodbye. They were good friends, so Kathy thought. Most of the time Tina liked Kathy but sometimes she would have nothing to do with Kathy. That hurt Kathy's feelings because she had done nothing to her but she would forgive her every time. She realized that Ken had done her a favor by walking out on her. She showed herself how strong she was and that she could take care of herself. Even though the pain was awful, it made her a stronger person. She had lots of friends and a strong family that helped her get through the first year that Ken was gone. After that it got alittle easier with each passing day. Kathy had adopted Ken's mama for her own and she was Kathy's rock besides God. She loved her as if she were her own mama. Then one real foggy morning, on their way to work in Quitman, they had a wreck. Charleen was driving but she was having to go slow because the fog was so thick that you couldn't see your hand in front of your face. When they topped the hill, there sat an eighteen wheeler across both sides of the road and in the driveway. Charleen turned towards the driveway hoping she could miss it but as they got closer to the last set of back tires, they knew they were going to hit them. Kathy was in front with Charleen and Tammy was in the back seat. They all had their seat belts on but Tammy. Kathy remembers seeing small pieces of metal flying and then everything went blank for a short while for all of them. When they came around, the eighteen wheeler had moved out of the road and was sitting all the way in the drive way. Charleen was scared the car was fixing to catch on fire. She couldn't get out of her door, so she climbed over Kathy. Tammy had come in between the two front seats and hit the rear view mirror but she had gotten out also. Kathy's seatbelt wouldn't unlock at first and that scared her because she wanted out too. After Charleen got out, Kathy's seat belt unlocked and she got out. But when she stood up, blood went to pouring from her face. Tammy screamed"I can't look at that. "Kathy didn't know what Tammy was talking about. By this time Kathy is getting hysterical because of so much blood. She's asking Charleen to help her. Charleen went to the trunk of the car and got out a roll of paper towels that they would use on the job. She would give Kathy wads of paper that would be full of blood in no time. Someone called 911 and Kathy called Ken. But he didn't care. He didn't come check on her. She don't know why she called him. The ambulance got there, put Kathy on a backboard and put her in the ambulance. The EMT told the other EMT that Kathy had a lasseration to the right side of her head but couldn't put to much gauze on it because of the neck brace they had put on her. Kathy hated the ambulance ride, it felt like she was going to fall and that she was hanging upside down at times. It scared her. Worst ride in her life.

She was glad to get to the hospital. That was her first ambulance ride and hoped that she wouldn't have to ride in one again. Her sisters were there when she got there. Louise worked there, so she got there before June did. When June got there, she had to walk back out. She cried at what she saw but she didn't want Kathy to see her cry. Kathy got to the hospital about eight that morning. She laid in the emergency room till that afternoon. Then she started hurting in her legs and her back after about a couple of hours. She begged them to take the backboard off her. But they couldn't till they did the CT scans. So, they got her in to do the CT scans when the pain got really bad. They found that her eye socket was broken in three places, her nose was broke, her cheek bone was broke in two places, the jaw bone was broke in two places on the left side of her face and she had a four inch gash on the right side of her head. But other than that she was okay. She wasn't in much pain after they finally took her off that backboard. They had brought Tammy in also, she was having labor pains. They gave her something and sent her home about six-thirty that afternoon. They finally put Kathy in a room about three that afternoon. Her sons were there and so was her ex-husband, Tim. Lee had called him. The wreck happened on a Thursday morning.

Kathy's face was so swollen on the left side and they were putting ice packs on it to get some of the swelling down, so they could do surgery on her. Louise gave her a mirror to look at because Kathy wanted to see the damage. She didn't realize how bad it looked till she saw it herself. Her hair was caked with dry blood. Louise tried to help Kathy wash her hair to try to get some of the blood out. Between the two, they were able to get alot of it out. If you looked, you could still see it in her hair. She had laid in the emergency room for five hours with her head bleeding before the doctor came in and put five staples in her head. She didn't need any thing for pain but at night she would ask for something, so she could sleep because she had to sleep sitting up, so that the ice pack would be against the left side of her face. The swelling went down enough that Dr. Vincient did the surgery on Monday. He had to put plates and screws in her cheek bones, her jaw bones, her eye socket and her temple area. He also put a brace on her nose. He also had to put a screen mesh square to hold up her left eye because the fatty tissue was gone that holds your eye in place. Dr. Vincient came in Tuesday morning to see how Kathy was doing. She ask him when she could go home and he told her if she felt like it and thought she could handle it, then she could go home that afternoon. Kathy was glad that she was going home. She felt alright and she wasn't in much pain. Never was in much pain at all and found that hard to believe as much damage as there was.

She could feel air hitting her eye when she breathed in threw her nose and the left side of her face was numb. It destoried her sinus's in her cheek and temple area. She was going to have to live with all that forever. But Dr. Vincient was a good plastic surgeon, that he made it look almost like it was suppose to. You can only tell it when Kathy takes her glasses off. June and Louise took Kathy home and got her settled in. Kathy was gonna sleep on the couch till she could lay her head on a pillow like she use to. As of now, she had to sleep like she did in the hospital bed. Her neighbor, Don would come over to see about her and bring her a plate for dinner and supper. Ken and Tina would bring her food, so she wouldn't have to cook. Her friends and family would come check on her. About two weeks after the surgery, Kathy had to go see Dr. Vincent, to get the staples out and the stitches took out from where he did surgery. He had to cut Kathy where her bottom lashes grew and it was very painful when he started taking them out. Kathy wanted to cry but couldn't.

Kathy's left eye was black from the wreck and surgery. Tim also came and checked on her. He still cared for her after twelve years of divorce. About a month after surgery, the left eye got infected and she had to go get some antibiotics. About three weeks later, a small yellow bump came up in the corner of her eye on the inside. She had to go back to Dr. Vincient. He had to put a shot in her eye to deaden it, so he could lance it and get all the infection out of it. Three months later, Kathy woke up crying with her eye. It felt like somebody had put sand in her eye and she couldn't ease it off. June carried her to an eye specialist. He ran some tests and found that Kathy's eye lid didn't blink like it was suppose to and that at night her eye lid would stay open, causing the eye to dry out. He told her that she would have to put eye salve in it at night and drops during the day for the rest of her life.

She couldn't afford to buy the medicine that she needed. June went through a company that put out eye drops and salve. She was able to get Kathy a years supply. About six months after the surgery, Kathy had to go back through surgery again because one of the plates that he had put in her jaw bone was coming through the gum. So Dr. Vincient, took that one plate out. Kathy's money was running low that she had saved. She called her lawyer and talked to him about her financial situation. He told her not to worry, that she could borrow from this company until she got her settlement. But she could only borrow every 45 days so she would borrow enough for two or three months.

So, Kathy would stay busy all week and on Saturday night, she would go out with the girls to the Vex dance hall. She looked for work and got a job but her eye bothered her so much that she couldn't hold it. She gave her boss man two weeks notice but he knew that her eye hurt so, he found a replacement for her within the week. Her and the girls went out every Saturday night for years. Kathy had stopped dating. She was having fun doing what she wanted and only taking care of herself. She got lonely sometimes but she would find something to keep her busy. She would make quilts. Kathy loved making them and everyone loved them. Kathy did meet someone and they connected but then something tragic happened in his life and his actions hurt Kathy. Kathy had felt that kind of pain enough so, she decided right then that she had been hurt enough and didn't want to feel that kind of pain again, so she threw herself into working on her house and going out with the girls. Her best friend, Loretta and her hit the Vex every Saturday night. They would dance so much they would be plum wore out but they had so much fun. Kathy didn't drink so she was their designated driver. One night at the Vex, Kathy met Laredo. He was different from any man she knew. He treated her like a lady. He ask her if he could come see her sometimes and she told him that she would like that. After that, they were inseperable. Laredo had two children, one boy and a girl. His daughter, Liz was living with him. His son, Steve was in the Air Force, stationed in Philidelphia. Kathy had custody of her grandson, Sam until Jessica got her life in order. Kathy and Sam loved going to Laredo's house. Laredo had horses, chickens and ducks. Sam loved the horses. Liz and Sam got along so good. Every Saturday night, Laredo would meet Kathy out at the Vex. All Kathy's friends thought the world of Laredo. He also had two other children that he adopted from his first wife.

Laredo planned a surprise birthday party for Kathy, on Friday night. All her friends came over and all her kids. It was the first real birthday party Kathy had ever had. She had a blast. She had always wanted a surprise birthday party. It was as she had always dreamed about.

Laredo had planned another special get together with friends and families the next day. When everyone got there, he gathered them around and said a pray. Then, Laredo got on one knee and ask Kathy to marry him. She was so happy and told him that she would. They set the date for the 19th of March. In the mean time, she had a meeting with her lawyer and a mediater, to see if they could come to some kind of an settlement. Which, after a couple of hours, they finally came to a settlement but it would be April first before she would get any money. She only had three months to get everything ready. Her future sister-n-law Emily, made the flower bouquets and bootneers. Her other sister-n-law to be made the wedding cake and Vicki, her other sister-n-law loaned Kathy her cow girl hat and veil. June ordered Kathy's western wedding dress off of EBay, for a really low price. Kathy and Laredo went to talk to Brother Jonas about him marrying them. Also to ask if they could use the church for their wedding and reception. Brother Jonas talk to them about their feelings and their plans for the future. He gave them permission to use the church and his blessing. On the morning of the 19th, Kathy went to the church to help her sister-n-laws put the wedding cake together and to get the church ready. Two o'clock was rapidly approaching and Kathy wasn't quite ready. She had to go back to Laredo's and get her wedding dress and all the flowers for the bridal party. Her brother, Bill was going to walk her down the aisle. Out of all the running around, Kathy forgot the music for the wedding. When it came time to start the wedding, someone had found a pretty song to play, so they could seat everyone. Then, it was time. The best man, Roger sang a beautiful song for the bride to walk down the aisle to. It was a beautiful wedding and reception. Laredo's best friend, Red Man's wife,

Leslie took all of the wedding pictures. They were beautiful. She had an eight by ten made like a cover of a magazine of a picture of Kathy as the bride of the month on it. Afterwards, they loaded everything in Kathy's car, forgetting that the bride and groom had to leave together. But Laredo rode home in his son's car and Kathy drove to Laredo's by herself. Everyone gathered at Laredo's house. Kathy, Laredo and all their friends realized that they had left in seperate cars, they had a good laugh about that. So, that was their first funny memory of their wedding day. Everyone partied for awhile and then left. Laredo and Kathy was going to leave to go to West Virginia that night but decided to wait and leave real early the next morning. Laredo was taking Kathy to see the only Mom that she had ever had in her life. She had not seen her in eight years. Kathy was so excited. Laredo was so good to her. She was really happy. Laredo was everything that she had ever dreamed of in a man. They got up and started their trip early. They stopped often and one place they did stop at was the worlds biggest flea market in Tennessee. Laredo bought her a purple stoned ring because that was her favorite color. They made it to her Mom's house about four that afternoon. Her and Mom sat up till two am talking. Kathy helped her mom get things low enough for her to reach. Kathy had so much fun with her mom and her mom loved Laredo, too. The whole family got together and cooked them a big supper. Everyone liked Laredo. They stayed for four days. They helped mom go through boxes and got garage sale items together. Mom also gave Kathy some tupperware items. Mom wanted the small room cleaned up and her room rearranged. She also wanted her shed cleaned out. After that, they started home. Kathy wanted to stay longer but she knew that they had to get back home. They had horses to tend to. Their lives together was happy. Liz lived with them for alittle while. Her and her husband were trying to work out their problems. After about a month, they got a trailer just outside of town. Kathy was so happy for Liz because she knew how much Liz loved her husband and had been praying that they would get back together. Laredo and Kathy were so happy. They spent every moment they could with one another. Kathy had always dreamed of a love like this but didn't think that it was real. Laredo made her feel so special and so loved. She was on top of the world and wanted to shout her love for Laredo for all to hear. The trucking company finally settled with her. She bought them a truck a piece, a tractor and a back hoe. His ex- wife had sold all his mowers and tractors, while he was on the road and he wasn't able to keep his place cleaned up like he use to. Now they would be able to really get the place cleaned up like it use to look. They worked hard to get it cleaned up and it was beginning to look like it did when Laredo first moved there.

They went on a weekend cruise and had a great time. Laredo hadn't been on one before. It was a gambling ship. They went on the top deck and watched the dolphins and jelly fish. They had fun but only played a small amount of money on the slot machines. They had got a motel room for the weekend. They went and seen Louise. They walked the beach for conch shells. That May 2011, a friend called her and told her to get a Lowndes paper. So, Kathy bought a paper and got upset with what she read. In the paper was the story of her Mama. The boy (that killed her Mama) sister had gave an interview. She was trying to get in touch with all the victims of the families that her brother had killed.

Kathy called her two sisters and her brother to tell them about the story in the paper. It had been fifty years since Kathy's mama had been murdered in cold blood. She had come to grips with the whole thing and had forgiven the boys for taking her mama from her. Now, it was all reopened again and for what, she could not understand.

Parker's sister wanted everyone to know how she had suffered. Kathy could not see how Parker's sisters pain was any worse than what he had put all the families through, especially what he had done to her and her siblings; when he killed his victims. She was devastated from the story that Parker's sister wrote. But from Parker's sisters story, she found out that all the murders could have been stopped. The two boys were awol soldiers. The military police had caught them at Parker's house, hiding under the porch. They dragged them out and took them back and locked them up again. Somehow they escaped again. They went back to his mama's house to tell his mother that they would be camping out at the river. His mother and sister would take them food, instead of turning them in, like they should have done. It wasn't like they were going to be shot or something, only just to do some time. If only they had done that, Kathy's life would not have been turned upside down. Kathy and her two sisters met with the reporter that had written the story. They all broke down and cried. The pain was still with them and probably would always be. Kathy and her sisters decided to tell their side of the story. Each one of the girls learned something that each of them had kept to themselves, that no one knew about. They cried as they told their story and what they had gone through and still go through sometimes. Louise was so upset because she had only been three months old at the time. Louise felt cheated of her mama, which she had been. They couldn't understand why the boys were not turned in for going awol. They realized how their lives would have been different and that their daddy would have been so much happier had the two boys been turned in for AWOL.

Their brother wanted to be there with them but couldn't get up there in time. He lived in Florida, several hours away. The reporter ask if they would be willing to meet Parker's sister, Kathy and Louise said they would try it but June said that she just could not. Kathy told the reporter how she had forgiven the boys because she wanted to go to Heaven and the only way was to forgive. June said she guess that she would go to hell because she couldn't forgive them. It was an emotional interview. All the old feelings came back on top of what they had kept to only themselves. Now each one of the girls knew what each one had endured. Louise never got to have a memory about her mama. Kathy only had flashes of memories, since she had blocked the first two or three years after her mama's death. So, their side of the story was put in the paper. Laredo was Kathy's rock and her mom. He held her and talked with her. The pain came back with the story. She was so glad that he was in her life. She called her mom and told her all about it. Her mom was as shocked as they all were that the sister wanted to meet with the families that her brother had killed a member of. Kathy was just glad that her daddy didn't have to go through any of it again. He had suffered so much at the hands of her brother, Parker. How could she justify what he had done?Now, they would have to try to put it behind them again. No one will ever really know what they went through, only them and the other victims and the good Lord. Kathy thanked God for her husband every day. The love that he showed her was awsome, since no one had shown her that kind of love before. He helped her through it all. In July, they went back up to West Virginia to the family reunion. They took her grandson, Sam with them. They had a blast. At the family reunion they had an auction of things that everyone brought. You had to bring a good gift and a gag gift. The gifts had to be wrapped so no one could see what they were. Sometimes it would be a bidding war and they would all laugh. They ate good food and had a great time visiting with all the family. They went up on a Friday and came home on a Sunday. Boy, was they tired but they had so much fun. Kathy and Laredo went on with their lives. Then one day, the owner of where Laredo worked decided to sell the business. The new owners started cutting hours and pay. Laredo didn't want Kathy going back to work, so he went back to driving an eighteen wheeler. He would be home on weekends and sometimes he would come close enough to where they lived that he would get to spend alittle time with Kathy during the week. That always made them both happy. Laredo hated being back on the road but if it kept Kathy from working, then that is what he had to do. Kathy was getting ready for Christmas. That was her favorite time of the year. She always cooked a big meal at Thanksgiving and Christmas, she loved doing that. It was a tradition she started in 1993. She wished that she had done that when her daddy was alive and that she had got him to come spend the night with them, so he could watch his grandchildren opening their presents. That was the only regret that she had where her daddy was concerned. Her Christmas tree was always full of presents. Their tree was real full that year. She had so much fun wrapping presents and couldn't hardly wait till Christmas. Kathy made alot of quilts for presents that year. Kathy got her mom's package ready and got it in the mail, so she would have presents to open on Christmas morning. She always sent her mom a package full of presents but she could only open them on Christmas morning. They had all the family and some friends over for dinner and gift exchanges. Everyone had so much fun. Kathy's life seemed so complete with Laredo. He would take her on moon lit walks or they would just sit outside in the afternoon and at night looking at the stars. They would talk about their plans for them to do together. He was her knight in shining armor and she was his beautiful little woman, as he tells her that all the time. She had never known a love like this and she was finally content with her life.